9/20

The Brave Cyclist

The True Story of a Holocaust Hero

by Amalia Hoffman

illustrated by Chiara Fedele

CAPSTONE EDITIONS

a capstone imprint

For the Friebrun and Einleger families. —A.H.

The Brave Cyclist is published by
Capstone Editions, a Capstone imprint
1710 Roe Crest Drive
North Mankato, Minnesota 56003
www.capstonepub.com

Library of Congress Cataloging-in-Publication
Names: Hoffman, Amalia, author.
Title: The brave cyclist : the true story of a Holocaust hero / by Amalia
Hoffman.
Description: North Mankato, Minnesota : Capstone Editions, [2020] |
Audience: Ages: 9-10. | Audience: Grades: 4-6.
Identifiers: LCCN 2019000202| ISBN 9781684460632 (hardcover) |
ISBN 9781684460649 (ebk. pdf)
Subjects: LCSH: Bartali, Gino, 1914–2000. | Cyclists—Italy—
Biography—Juvenile literature. | World War, 1939–1945—Jews—
Rescue—Italy—Juvenile literature.
Classification: LCC GV1051.B37 H64 2020 | DDC 796.6/2092 [B]—dc23
LC record available at https://lccn.loc.gov/2019000202

Photo credits: Newscom/Splash News/New Press Photo, 38

Book design by Brann Garvey

Printed and bound in the United States of America.
002533

"If you're good at a sport, they attach the medals to your shirts and then they shine in some museum. That which is earned by doing good deeds is attached to the soul and shines elsewhere."

—Gino Bartali

Gino Bartali clutched the handlebars. Too short for Papa's bike, he shifted from side to side like a clumsy *pinguino*. His friends giggled, but Gino worried only about keeping his balance.

Pedaling along the bank of the Arno River in Italy, he dreamed of cycling on a shiny bike of his own.

Mama and Papa could hardly scrape together enough money to pay for food and clothes. When Gino turned 12, he spent his summer working to earn money for a bike. He could find only a boring job: helping farmers shred dried palm-tree leaves into strings used for weaving baskets.

When summer ended—and with a few extra *lira* that his family chipped in—Gino had just enough money to buy a rusty old bike.

Despite being small and sickly, Gino often led his friends on a steep, daring climb. The slope was called *Moccoli*, which means "Curses."

Gino was amazed that he could easily outrace his friends to the top even though they were bigger and stronger.

From there Gino could look down on the city of Florence with its cathedrals, palazzos, and the grand synagogue.

Gino wanted to learn more about cycling. As a sixth grader, he took a part-time job at a bike shop. The shop owner, Oscar Casamonti, repaired racing bikes. He also competed in local races.

Although Gino had a hard time concentrating on schoolwork, he listened attentively as Casamonti explained how to repair punctured tires, adjust brakes, and fix broken frames.

One day Casamonti invited Gino to join him and his fellow racers on a ride. The cyclists pedaled through the Tuscan hills surrounding the village of Ponte a Ema, where Gino lived.

Some riders dropped out along the way, but Gino kept going.

Casamonti was so impressed that he urged Gino's parents to let the boy compete in professional races.

At first Papa and Mama refused. They worried that the sport was too dangerous. And Gino had always been so frail and weak!

But Gino kept pleading.

Finally, on Gino's 17th birthday in July 1931, Papa gave in and granted his son the best birthday wish ever—permission to enter races and compete against other cyclists for awards.

Gino's heart sped up. He had won Papa's trust. Now he must make himself into a winner.

Each morning as the rooster crowed, Gino rose to perform 24 exercises. He trained to strengthen his muscles. He learned to slow down his breathing while riding long distances.

Gino taught himself how to switch between sitting on the bike and standing on the pedals. He experimented with different diets to see which helped him the most. During one race, he gobbled up a dozen raw eggs, cracking their shells on his handlebars as he rode.

By age 21 the frail boy had turned into a powerful racer.

When Gino joined a racing team, he had to prove himself as a *gregario*. That's a rider who must do everything to help his team's leader win the race. Gino carried water bottles and changed tires on the road for the other cyclists. Soon he gained respect and became the captain of his own team.

Gino participated in races across Italy. In 1936 he won his country's most prestigious competition—the Giro d'Italia—and earned enough money to buy a home for his parents.

But Gino's wheels kept spinning for more. The most important event in the cycling world was the Tour de France. For many miles and many days, riders raced through France's most monstrous mountains. In 1938 Gino was ready for the challenge.

Racing on rugged roads, Gino charged up jagged, grueling slopes in the Pyrenees mountain range. Pain penetrated his muscles, but he kept climbing until he reached the highest peak.

But as Gino swooped downhill, he noticed that some spectators had stepped into the road to cross over to the other side. Gino was terrified that he might hit them, so he clenched the brakes. He was thrown from his bike and flew into the air.

Gino crashed to the ground, suffering scrapes, cuts, and bruises to his arms and legs. His bike ended up in a tangle, its front wheel crushed.

As pain throbbed from his hips to his chest, Gino counted the seconds as he waited for a replacement for the damaged wheel. When his crew finally finished the work, he gathered his strength to get back on the bike in spite of the pain.

Gino pressed on but couldn't make up for lost time. The Belgian riders had passed him. He wouldn't win that stage of the race.

But 15 days remained in the tour. Gino was determined not to be defeated by the crash.

Gino fought to take the lead once again. His pulse pounded as he attacked the dirt and gravel course, storming up and down the high summits of the Alps, speeding toward victory.

Declared "King of the Mountains," Gino got to wear the yellow jersey, an honor reserved for the winner of each daily stage. He kept the yellow jersey all the way to the finish line in Paris.

As Gino rode into the stadium there, reporters and photographers crowded around him while thousands of spectators cheered him on.

But Gino feared that the taste of victory would be bittersweet. There was trouble back in Italy.

At that time the Italian prime minister, Benito Mussolini, had declared himself *Il Duce*, meaning simply "The Leader." Anyone daring to disagree with him risked severe punishment. Mussolini decided who should compete in sporting competitions. Champions were expected to praise and thank him to show their loyalty.

After winning the Tour de France, it was Gino's turn to speak to the crowds in Paris.

Gino thanked his coach, saying, "During a moment when my legs started to become heavy or I felt that burning in my stomach . . . I heard your voice . . . and then soon enough, I felt myself comforted."

Later, speaking over the radio, Gino thanked his fans and teammates but didn't mention Mussolini.

Gino's speech angered the authorities back in Italy. The hero who had fought so hard to win the world's greatest bicycling competition would receive no grand reception when he returned to his country.

In July 1938 Mussolini published a hateful document declaring that Jewish citizens were enemies of the state. Jewish children were expelled from public schools and couldn't play in public parks. Their parents were often forced out of their jobs.

Mussolini teamed with the German leader, Adolf Hitler, who declared similar laws in Germany. Many Jewish people who were not born in Italy were dragged out of their homes and even arrested.

Jewish people were forced to carry documents bearing their photographs, names, and signatures at all times. That way soldiers could identify them.

As World War II raged into the autumn of 1943, Gino received a mysterious telephone call.

The call came from Gino's good friend, Cardinal Elia Dalla Costa, the archbishop of the church in Florence. The cardinal wanted to meet Gino in private.

When Gino arrived at Dalla Costa's office, the cardinal closed the door behind them. Then, in a hushed voice, he explained a secret plan.

Dalla Costa wanted to save Jewish people in Italy by supplying them with false identification cards so they could escape to safety.

Two skilled printers from the city of Assisi, Luigi and Trento Brizi, had already agreed to secretly print the documents. They would use real photographs but change the addresses, places of birth, and signatures, giving each Jewish person a non-Jewish name and a new identity.

The cardinal wanted to know if Gino would help them.

Gino was puzzled. The only jobs he'd ever had were those of farmhand, bike mechanic, and bike racer. How could he help?

The cardinal explained how Gino could use his bike for something even more daring than racing up and down the steepest mountains.

Gino knew that helping Jewish people was a crime punishable by imprisonment or even death. Still, he agreed to be a secret courier for the cardinal. Gino would risk his safety to help people he'd never met.

Early one morning Gino picked up documents from Dalla Costa's assistant in Florence. The papers included photos of Jewish people and their identification cards. After removing the seat and its post from the bike, Gino hid the documents inside the hollow bicycle frame.

Then he sped off to deliver them to the printers in the town of Assisi. The trip of some 110 miles would not be an easy one. On the road, soldiers halted Gino at a checkpoint. His heart raced. Surely his bike would be searched! Gino feared what the men might do to him if they discovered his secret cargo.

The soldiers recognized Gino as the beloved Italian champion cyclist. He used his fame to his advantage.

Gino asked the soldiers not to touch his bike and made up an excuse. The distance between his seat, handlebars, and pedals had to be precise to avoid a muscle strain, he explained. The soldiers believed him.

Gino wiped the sweat off his forehead and continued his journey.

When he arrived in Assisi, Gino delivered the documents from the cardinal's assistant. In exchange, he picked up the forged identification cards that Luigi and Trento Brizi had prepared. The new identification cards bore non-Jewish names. Gino hoped that the precious documents would save Jewish people.

He hid them in his bike and hurried back to Florence.

Along the way, Gino spotted an army patrol. He steered onto a side road and hid in the bushes.

When daylight faded, he spotted glowing lights in the dark. Worried they could be the headlights of military motorcycles, he rubbed mud all over his bike's frame. That way the chrome wouldn't shine in the light of an oncoming vehicle.

For months, Gino encountered new obstacles with each mission. He rode with many questions on his mind. Could he convince the soldiers that his frequent trips were solely for training purposes? What if he couldn't get back in time to deliver the documents? What would happen to the people whose lives depended on him?

The faces of innocent people in the photographs he smuggled reminded Gino that his mission was worthy of any sacrifice. He became more determined with each trip.

Gino couldn't predict what would happen in his war-ridden country. Danger filled each day in Italy. Once, when Gino stopped for coffee, a burst of machine gun fire almost hit his bike.

In 1944 Gino's worst fear came true. Il Duce's authorities discovered some letters from the church in Rome, thanking Gino for his good work.

The authorities didn't know what Gino had done, but they accused him of selling guns to groups fighting against Mussolini. Il Duce's men locked Gino in a dark cell. Sitting on a filthy floor, he heard the screams of prisoners being beaten. Gino was questioned for three days. He finally convinced the squad that he hadn't delivered guns but only helped to provide food for the poor.

Freed from jail but anxious and shaken, Gino worried that he would not be able to continue his important work.

One day he heard a shrieking blast. The Germans were blowing up most of the bridges around Florence. They wanted to slow down the British forces that were advancing toward the city in the effort to defeat Hitler and Mussolini.

On August 11, 1944, the bells rang out over the Bargello, the People's Palace in Florence. As Jewish people crept out of their hiding places and joined crowds dancing in the streets, Gino heard the news. More than four years of war, terror, and hardship had come to an end.

Gino had prayed that Mussolini and Hitler would be defeated. Now his prayers had been answered. After months of hiding, trembling, and concealing his secret, Gino joined the happy crowd. Italians were free of their dictator and safe from war.

Soon Gino shined up his bike.

Though peace had finally returned, the effects of war remained. Women scurried around, searching for scraps of food. Children played in the rubble of destroyed buildings.

Gino was determined to lift up the spirits of his fellow Italians. He began planning his next race. At age 34, he was considered *il vecchio*, an old man, in the sport of cycling. Many fans wondered if Gino could compete against much younger riders.

But Gino trained with fierce determination, just as he had in his youth.

In 1948, caked in mud and soaked by rain, he won the Tour de France for the second time. People of all races and religions celebrated. Neither poverty nor hardship could weaken their spirits.

The frail, sickly boy who once struggled to ride his papa's bike had restored Italians' faith in freedom and justice.

Afterword

Gino Giovanni Bartali was born July 18, 1914. He lived with his parents, sisters, and brother in Ponte a Ema, Italy. His father was a laborer and his mother earned extra money by tending to crops and embroidering lace.

Gino was particularly close to his younger brother, Giulio, who was also an accomplished cyclist. Sadly, Giulio died in 1936 after his bicycle collided with a car. Gino was devastated.

In 1940 Gino married Adriana Bani. They had two sons, Andrea and Luigi, and a daughter, Bianca Maria. So, while helping those in need during the war, Gino risked not only his life but the safety of his family.

Cardinal Dalla Costa contacted Gino after the cardinal agreed to aid members of Delasem. This organization was founded by courageous people of all religions, committed to rescuing Italian Jews as well as those who fled to Italy from other countries during World War II. Many priests, nuns, and clergy assisted Delasem by hiding and feeding Jewish people.

When Gino agreed to transport photographs and false identification cards, he was instructed not to make contact with any of the Jewish people who received them. He couldn't share information with anyone—not even his wife. And he knew nothing of others carrying papers to help Jewish people. That way, if he were caught, others would not be at risk.

Gino Bartali

Besides his role as a secret courier, Gino also rescued a Jewish friend, Giacomo Goldenberg, by helping the Goldenberg family hide in an apartment in Florence that Gino co-owned. At a time when his family had hardly enough to eat, he delivered food to the Goldenbergs, knowing that their situation was even worse.

For most of his later life, Gino didn't reveal much about his heroic activities during the war and often refused to be interviewed by newspaper or television reporters who wanted to tell his story. He believed that his being a famous athlete would overshadow the contributions of the many other people who risked their lives to help those in need.

"I don't want to appear to be a hero," he said. "Heroes are those who died, who were injured, who spent many months in jail."

Gino died May 5, 2000, at the age of 85.

His legend lives on in Italy. The Gino Bartali Cycling Museum opened in 2006 in his hometown of Ponte a Ema. The museum features Gino's bicycles along with photographs and other Bartali memorabilia. In the same year, the Italian president, Carlo Ciampi, posthumously awarded Gino and four priests gold medals for their bravery during the war.

An annual cycling journey in Italy, called *ciclo pelegrinaggio*, was launched in 2009 to retrace part of Gino's smuggling route between Florence and Assisi.

In 2013 Gino was recognized by Yad Vashem, the Holocaust Museum in Jerusalem, Israel, as a Righteous Among the Nations. This honor is bestowed on non-Jews who risked their lives to save Jewish people during the Holocaust. Cardinal Dalla Costa, along with brave printers Luigi and Treno Brizi (who were father and son), was also awarded the honor.

The legend of the brave cyclist lives on with a bicycle race in Jerusalem and a bicycle path at the Haruvit Forest near Jerusalem, which was established in Gino's honor in 2018.

Creators

Amalia Hoffman is an author, illustrator, and storyteller. Her board book *Dreidel Day* was selected as a PJ Library book and received the PJ Library Author Incentive Award. Two board books, *Astro Pea* and *All Colors*, followed in 2019. Her other books include *The Klezmer Bunch* and *Purim Goodies*. Amalia designed and illustrated *Rose Bud*, an oversized book with pop-up elements, for Israel's children's theater, The Train. Her article "Queen Esther and I" was published in *Highlights Magazine for Children* in March 2016. Amalia grew up in Jerusalem, Israel, and now resides in Westchester, New York. She frequently presents her books in schools, libraries, bookstores, and community centers. Visit Amalia at www.amaliahoffman.com.

Chiara Fedele attended art school in Milan, Italy, completing a degree in illustration at La Scuola del Fumetto. A freelance illustrator since 2004, she has created art for several children's books and has provided illustrations for use in movies, advertising, and magazines. She also teaches at the International Schools of Comics in the Italian cities of Padova, Brescia, and Genova. Chiara now lives with her family in a small village about 50 kilometers from her home city of Milan.

Select Bibliography

Bosworth, R.J.B. *Mussolini's Italy*. New York: The Penguin Press, 2006.

Cheetham, Nicolas, and Matt Rendell. *The Official Tour De France 1903-2004*. London: Weidenfeld & Nicolson, 2004.

Crutchely, Peter. *Gino Bartali: The Cyclist Who Saved Jews in Wartime Italy*. Belfast: BBC, May 9, 2014.

De Felice, Renzo. *The Jews in Fascist Italy*. New York: Enigma Books, 2001.

Fife, Graeme. *Tour de France: The History, The Legend, The Riders*. Edinburgh and London: Mainstream Publishing, 2011.

Gilbert, Martin. *The Second World War: A Complete History*. New York: Henry Holt and Company, 1989.

My Italian Secret: The Forgotten Heroes of the Holocaust. Directed by Oren Jacoby. Arlington, VA: PBS Distribution, 2015.

McConnon, Aili and Andres. *Road to Valor*. New York: Random House, 2012.

Ramati, Alexander. *The Assisi Underground: The Priests Who Rescued Jews*. Briarcliff, NY: Stein and Day/Scarborough House, 1978.

Rendell, Matt. *Blazing Saddles—The Cruel and Unusual History of the Tour De France*. Boulder, CO: Velo Press, 2008.

Sinai, Alon. "Long Overdue Honor for Righteous Christian Italian Cycling Great Bartali," *The Jerusalem Post*, October 8, 2013.

Startt, James. *Tour De France/Tour De Force*. San Francisco: Chronicle Books, 2000.

Thompson, S. Christopher. *The Tour De France*. Berkeley and Los Angeles: University of California Press, 2006.

Source Notes

"If you're good at a sport. . ." Aili and Andres McConnon. *Road to Valor*. New York: Random House, p. 245.

"During a moment when. . ." Ibid., p. 84.

"I don't want to appear. . ." Ibid., p. 244.